Your Very Own Russian Dolls!

In this book, you'll discover dozens of beautiful dolls and patterns ready for you to doodle and decorate. Use felt-tip pens to colour and draw, but leave them to dry to make sure they don't smudge. Then just add the right stickers from the middle of the book.

Have fun!

Scholastic Children's Books,
Euston House, 24 Eversholt Street,
London NW1 1DB, UK

A division of Scholastic Ltd
London ~ New York ~ Toronto ~ Sydney ~ Auckland
Mexico City ~ New Delhi ~ Hong Kong

Edited by Catharine Robertson

Published in the UK by Scholastic Ltd, 2014

Illustrated by Jillian Phillips
© Scholastic Children's Books, 2014

ISBN 978 1407 14535 8

Printed in Malaysia.

2 4 6 8 10 9 7 5 3 1

Papers used by Scholastic Children's Books are made from woods grown in sustainable forests.

Russian Roses

Use felt-tip pens and the special stickers from the middle of the book to complete this family of beautiful Russian dolls.

Home, Sweet Home

It's perfectly cosy inside this warm log cabin. Complete the scene with felt-tip pens, then use stickers to add extra-special touches.

Colour in the pretty Russian rose pattern
on the left, and then create your own
pattern with felt-tip pens and stickers here.

Nesting Dolls

Russian dolls are sometimes called nesting dolls because they can fit inside each other. Find the stickers that match these dolls inspired by St Basil's Cathedral in Russia, then use your felt-tip pens to colour them in.

Complete the scene! Use your felt-tip pens to add bright and beautiful colours to the fireworks and domes of St Basil's Cathedral in Moscow.

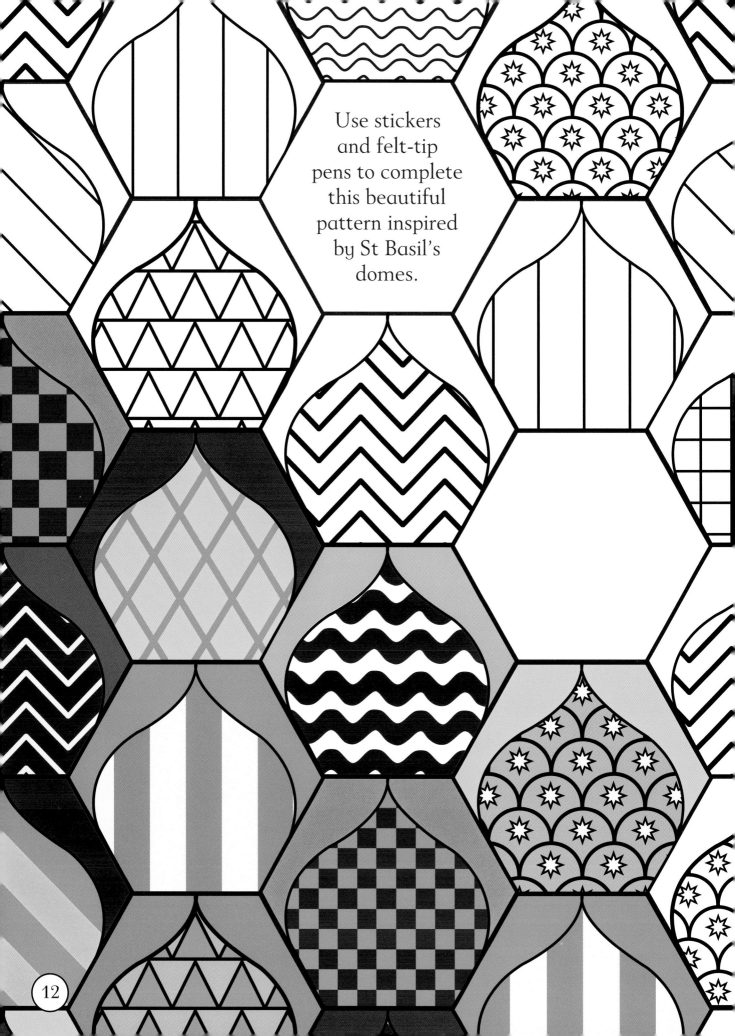

Use stickers and felt-tip pens to complete this beautiful pattern inspired by St Basil's domes.

Get Your Skates On

Use stickers from the middle of the book to give these wintry Russian dolls the perfect look for ice skating.

Use felt-tip pens to colour and doodle this traditional Russian pattern.

Russian Roses

(pages 2 and 3)

Home, Sweet Home

(pages 4 and 5)

Rose Pattern (page 7)

Nesting Dolls (pages 8 and 9)

St Basil's Pattern

(pages 12 and 13)

Get Your Skates On

(pages 14 and 15)

Ice Skating
(pages 18 and 19)

Ballet Dolls
(pages 20 and 21)

The Nutcracker (pages 22 and 23)

Snowy Dolls
(pages 26 and 27)

Sleigh Ride
(pages 28 and 29)

Cosy Quilt
(pages 30 and 31)

Here's another beautiful Russian pattern to colour and complete.

Ice Skating

The dolls have gone ice skating on a frozen lake. Use your stickers to complete this snowy skating scene.

Ballet Dolls

Use stickers from the middle of the book to decorate these Russian dolls and get them ready for a night at the ballet.

The Nutcracker

The dolls are watching a famous ballet called *The Nutcracker*. Use your stickers to finish the scenery and the ballet dancers' costumes.

Use felt-tip pens to colour this pattern of beautiful ballerinas.

Snowy Dolls

Doodle and colour in the beautiful snowy patterns on these dolls, and then use snowflake stickers to complete their outfits and the background.

Sleigh Ride

The dolls are taking a ride in a Russian sleigh. Use stickers from the middle of the book to finish the snowy scene.

Cosy Quilt

Keep warm on a snowy winter's night with this cosy patchwork quilt. Decorate it with felt-tip pens and stickers from the middle of the book.

Colour in these Russian dolls to make them bright and bold.